Heart of a Lion

THE LEADERSHIP SKILLS OF MEDAL OF HONOR
RECIPIENT LT. MICHAEL P. MURPHY, U.S. NAVY SEAL

Gary Williams

LAKOTA PRESS
West Chester, OH

Lakota Press
P.O. Box 531
West Chester, OH 45071

©2012 by Gary Williams
ISBN: 978-0-9848351-0-2 (e-book)
ISBN: 978-0-9848351-2-6 (softcover)

Requests for permission should be sent to Lakota Press, P.O. Box 531, West Chester, OH 45071or by e-mail to permissions@lakotapress.com.

The Lakota Press offers discounts on its titles when ordered in bulk for training, educational or fund-raising purposes. For more information, please contact the publisher directly by e-mail at sales@lakotapress.com or visit www.lakotapress.com.

Cover portrait by Gerald Slater
Cover design by Brian Ireson

To Medal of Honor recipient (posthumous) Navy SEAL LT. Michael P. Murphy and all of this nation's warriors past and present who defend our constitutional liberty, freedom, and American way of life.

ALSO BY GARY WILLIAMS

Siege in Lucasville:
The 11-Day Saga of Hostage Larry Dotson
(Bloomington, IN: Author House, 2003)

Siege in Lucasville:
An Insider's Account and Critical Review of Ohio's
Worst Prison Riot
(Bloomington, IN: Author House, 2006)

SEAL of Honor:
Operation Red Wings and the Life of LT. Michael P.
Murphy, USN,
(Annapolis: Naval Institute Press, 2010)

CONTENTS

SEAL of Honor: Operation Red Wings and the Life of LT. Michael P. Murphy, USN

Lieutenant Michael Patrick Murphy, a Navy SEAL, earned the Medal of Honor on 28 June 2005 for his bravery during a fierce fight with the Taliban in the remote mountains of eastern Afghanistan. The first to receive this nation's highest military honor for service in Afghanistan, Lieutenant Murphy was also the first naval officer to earn the medal since the Vietnam War, and the first SEAL to be honored posthumously. He was a young man, who was noted by his peers for his compassion and for his leadership which was guided by an extraordinary sense of duty, responsibility, and moral clarity.

Tracing Lieutenant Murphy's journey from a seemingly ordinary life on New York's Long Island to that remote mountainside half a world away, *SEAL of Honor* will help readers understand how he came to demonstrate the extraordinary heroism and selfless leadership that earned him our nation's highest military honor. Moreover, the book brings the Afghan war back to the home front, focusing on Lieutenant Murphy's tightly knit family and the devastating effect of his death upon them as they watched the story of Operation Red Wings unfold in the news. The book attempts to answer why his service to his country was a calling faithfully answered, a duty justly upheld, and a life, while all too short, well lived. *SEAL of Honor: Operation Red Wings and the Life of LT. Michael P. Murphy, USN* is published by the Naval Institute Press and available wherever books are sold.

Hardcover ISBN: 978-1591149576
Softcover ISBN: 978-1591149651
Visit www.sealofhonor.com

PREFACE

The foundation for this work lies in my study and development of the midlevel leadership program for the Ohio Department of Rehabilitation and Correction. My favorite authors regarding leadership are Donald T. Phillips, John Maxwell, and the late Jim Rohn. Phillips' *Lincoln on Leadership* and Maxwell's *The 21 Irrefutable Laws of Leadership* are found on many military and professional reading program lists, and the works of Jim Rohn most certainly should be. His books, lectures, and resource materials rank among the best in the industry, and I have relied on his work extensively. Another very important title demonstrating leadership in action is former New York City mayor Rudolph "Rudy" Giuliani's *Leadership*. I have read these titles several times and glean something new with each rereading.

ACKNOWLEDGMENTS

I would like to express my sincere gratitude to the family of Navy SEAL LT. Michael P. Murphy. The opportunity they have given me is more than I could have ever imagined. It has been more than a year since *SEAL of Honor: Operation Red Wings and the Life of LT. Michael P. Murphy, USN* was released, and during that time I have met thousands of active-duty military, veterans, spouses, widows, and family members of those who gave all in the defense of freedom.

I have had the honor and privilege of addressing dozens of military and veteran groups and military support groups, as well as visiting military hospitals and bases. One cannot make these visits and not be humbled by the character, service, and sacrifice, and inspired by the strength, courage, and commitment, of each individual. Any time you begin to thank those who have become such an integral part of "Team Murphy," you inevitably run the risk of omitting someone. That is certainly not my intent.

My wife, Tracy, and children—Aaron, Lisa, Bryan, David, Daniel, and Stephen—continue to serve as a source of pride and encouragement for me. They, along with my mother, Charlene, and siblings—Richard, Kevin, Julie, and Darin—remain my biggest advocates.

Kim Wolfert assumed the multiple roles of publicist, personal assistant, travel agent, project organizer, and social network administrator long before I realized I needed them. Quiet, unassuming, meticulous, and the ultimate "multitasker," she is truly the glue that bonds Team Murphy.

Adam Turner and I have become fast and lasting friends. His unending knowledge regarding information technology, graphic design, and the use and advantages of electronic platforms have proved to be essential.

Brig. Gen. Anthony J. Tata, United States Army (Ret.), an accomplished author and military expert, was one of our early advocates. A decorated military commander who fought Taliban leader Ahmad Shah for the same ground as Lieutenant Murphy, he provided a keen insight that proved to be invaluable. General Tata's highly successful military trilogy—*Sudden Threat*, *Rogue Threat*, and *Hidden Threat*—has resulted in his being hailed as the "new Tom Clancy."

I would also like to thank the professionals at the Naval Institute Press, and the patriots of the Military Order of the Purple Heart for their support. Along with the Navy League's Drew Bisset and John Groenveld, all have become invaluable extended members of our team.

I have had the honor of addressing hundreds of this nation's future warriors at our armed forces' service academies. They stand on the shoulders of those who have gone before, and I am confident that they are up to the unique challenges our nation faces.

INTRODUCTION

While conducting the research for and during the writing of *SEAL of Honor: Operation Red Wings and the Life of LT. Michael P. Murphy, USN*, I noticed that the leadership qualities of LT. Michael Murphy mirrored many of the leadership qualities described in the books referenced in the preface. In September 2010, during the promotional tour for *SEAL of Honor*, I met Capt. Reed Bonadonna, USMC, director of ethics and character development at the United States Merchant Marine Academy; Rear Adm. Mark Kenny, USN (Ret.), vice president of the Irregular Warfare Program at Northrup-Grumman; Vice Adm. Jon W. Craine, USN (Ret.), president of the State University of New York Maritime College; and the Central Pennsylvania Council of the Navy League of the United States. It is with their encouragement and recommendation that this work is published.

The information contained in the following pages is only for those who are serious about developing and maximizing their leadership skills. I understand that there may be some who will disagree with the information that follows. I would encourage you to read and process my argument before judging its validity or value. There will be plenty of time later to debate my conclusions.

Leadership is intangible, and therefore no weapon ever designed can replace it.

—Gen. Omar Bradley
Command & General Staff College

1

INFLUENCE, CHARACTER, AND INTEGRITY

Over the course of his short life, Michael Patrick Murphy came to personify three critically important pillars of leadership. First, before you can lead, you must positively influence others. Second, you must develop an unshakable moral character. Third, you must always act with integrity consistent with that character. To be sure, there are leaders who lack numbers two and three, but we are not talking about position-only leadership; we are talking about an integrity and character that transcends position-only leadership and provides the all-important moral authority to lead.

Influence

Influence can be described as the ability one individual has to alter or affect the behavior or attitude of another. Everyone has influence. The two key questions are, how much, and what kind?

When you were a child, I am certain that your parents inquired as to who your friends were and with whom you were spending your time. And I am as equally sure that at some point your parents said of one of your friends, "I don't want you hanging around with him or her because you will turn out just like them. They are a bad influence." As in most cases, our parents were correct.

Maybe some of your friend's parents said that about you. The good news is that even if you have had a negative influence on others in the past, you can change that. The important thing to remember is that you don't have to be in a high-profile position to be a person of influence. The fact that your life connects with others places you in a position to influence others. However, as John Maxwell and Jim Dornan related in their book *Becoming a Person of Influence*, "Influence is a curious thing. Even though we have an impact on nearly everyone around us, our level of influence is not the same with everyone." And depending on your actions and attitude, your influence can be positive or negative—adding or detracting value from other people's lives.

American poet and philosopher Ralph Waldo Emerson said, "Every man is a hero and an oracle to somebody, and to that person, whatever he says has an enhanced value." Before you can lead, you must influence. The good thing is that if your life connects with other people in any way, you have influence. If your goal is to lead others, you must gain their trust; but before you can gain their trust, you must be able to positively influence them. No one will follow an individual he or she does not trust. In his audio program *Take Charge of Your Life*, Jim Rohn said that when it comes to influence:

> You must constantly ask yourself these questions: Who am I around? What are they doing to me? What have they got me reading? Where do they have me going? What do they have me thinking? And, most important, what do they have me becoming? Then ask yourself the big question: Is that okay?

Character

In another of his works, *Cultivating an Unshakable Character;* Jim Rohn reminded us that the word *character* is derived from the Greek word meaning "chisel" or "the mark left by a chisel." A sharpened steel tool, a chisel is used to carve hard materials such as granite or marble. A chisel can also be used to strip away excess or unwanted materials, allowing us to get down to the essential material that can be sculpted. Rohn advocates that we must chisel our character out of the raw material with which we were born, and that everything that happens to us presents an opportunity to develop our character.

Character is never created by accident; it is only created by the conscious process of design, the result of the thousands of decisions that change who we are into the person we want to be. As I noted in *SEAL of Honor*,

> During the summer of Michael's junior year . . . his uncle . . . lost his battle with cancer and left his wife and three daughters. Their mother was incapable of caring for them, and the three girls . . . faced being placed in foster care. This was unacceptable to Dan and Maureen [Michael's parents], so the three girls came to live with the Murphys.
>
> As Maureen tried to set up sleeping arrangements, Michael approached her and insisted, "Mom, I have the biggest room. Put the girls in my room and I'll move to the sewing room. It's no big deal." With that Michael moved to the sewing room, the smallest in the house, without complaint.

In his description of character, Jim Rohn says,

> Character isn't something you are born with like your fingerprints; it's something you weren't born with

and must take responsibility for making . . . Like the burning bush in the Book of Exodus, the bush that burned but was not consumed by the flames; character sustains itself and nurtures itself—even as it is being tested, used, and challenged.

In an e-mail communication with the author, Michael was described by his cousin Kristen as

[A]lways humble. He was talented in every sport he played, and was considered a "team player," was dedicated, motivated, and put his team interests before his own personal pursuits. Mike did what was best for all involved, rather than choose to put himself in the spotlight. He was brighter than anyone knew, more athletic than we considered, more driven than we could have imagined. He was funny, had a sharp wit, intelligent sense of humor, and was always ready for a prank, but fiercely loyal to those he loved.

Character isn't created in a crisis; it only comes to light. As quoted in the Army's collection *Leadership Statements and Quotes*, during his address to the Citadel's 1979 graduating class, Vice Adm. James B. Stockdale, a former prisoner of war and a recipient of the Medal of Honor, said, "The test of character is not 'hanging in' when you expect light at the end of the tunnel, but performance of duty and persistence of example when you know no light is coming."

In SEAL of Honor, I noted that

> Through his father's [Dan's] career as a prosecuting attorney, Michael was able to see both the good and bad in people, and that even "bad" people can do good things while "good" people can do bad things . . .
>
> On occasion Michael accompanied his father to work, where he was able to observe criminal court proceedings firsthand. One particular day, he watched his father argue before the United States District Court for the Eastern District of New York. After the long day in court, Michael asked his father if he had won or lost. Dan responded, 'Michael, it's not winning or losing so much as justice being served and the truth being decided.' That answer stayed with Michael and later appeared on his law school applications.

In talking with dozens of individuals who knew Michael Murphy, many different nouns and adjectives were used to describe him; not surprisingly, uncompromising integrity was included in everyone's description.

As recorded in *Leadership Statements and Quotes*, during Gen. John Vessey Jr.'s remarks at the Naval War College, Newport, Rhode Island, on June 24, 1983, he admonished the graduating class:

> Inseparable from the concept of service is the concept of integrity. The citizens of this great Nation place great trust in their military services. They will continue to judge us by stricter rules than they apply to themselves and they should do that because, ultimately, their security rests with us and the way we perform our duties. The people of this Nation have entrusted their Armed Forces with the most awesome weapons the world has ever seen, but they have also placed the lives of their sons and daughters who serve and the safety of their own families for now and in the future in the hands of the Armed Forces. Don't confuse integrity with infallibility. There's a great tendency to do that. As Gary Cooper said in

High Noon, you should 'aim to be high-regarded'; but you should also remember that you are human and fallible. Those who will lead you are also human and fallible. The code of the warrior class has room for fallibility certainly. The higher up the flagpole you go, the more of your backside will show. There is room for that; but, there is no room for a lack of integrity or for those who place self before duty or self before comrades or self before country. Careerism is the one great sin, and it has no place among you. If you achieve success over the bodies or the careers of your comrades, you have served your nation poorly and you have violated the code of the warrior class.

There won't be any tribunal to judge your actions at the height of battle; there are only the hopes of the citizenry who are relying upon your integrity and skill. They may well criticize you later amid the relative calm of victory or defeat. But, there is a crucial moment in crisis or battle when those you lead and the citizens of the nation can only trust that you are doing what is right. And you develop that concept through integrity.

One day while in middle school, Michael Murphy and his young friend Paul received their grades from an exam taken earlier. After school, Michael's mother, Maureen, asked Paul and Michael how they had done on the exam. Paul was very excited, stating that he had received a 92. When Maureen asked Michael how he had done, he replied, "Oh, I did OK." Later that evening at the dinner table, the conversation turned to the exam, and when again asked by his mother how he had done on it, Michael stated that he had received a 96. When asked why he had not told her his score earlier, he simply replied, 'Mom, Paul was so excited about his 92, telling him my score would just have thrown cold water on him, so I didn't say anything. It was not that important.' Maureen relates that she has never forgotten that conversation. Even in elementary school, to Michael Murphy, it was never about him, but always about others.

Integrity

Integrity is derived from the Latin adjective *integer*, meaning "whole" or "complete." Used in this context, we can define it as the inner sense of "wholeness" derived from qualities such as honesty and consistency of character. We may conclude that others "have integrity" when we see that their actions are consistent with the values, beliefs, and principles they claim to hold. Integrity is the constant pursuit of the truth, and people of integrity are willing to pay the cost of truth.

In their book *Becoming a Person of Influence*, authors John Maxwell and Jim Dornan describe the essential characteristics of a successful person of influence. Uncompromising integrity topped the list. They explain:

> Integrity is your best friend. It will never betray you or put you in a compromising position. It keeps your priorities right. When you're tempted to take shortcuts, it helps you stay the right course. When others criticize you unfairly, it helps you keep going and take the high road of not striking back. And when others' criticism is valid, integrity helps you accept what they say, learn from it, and keep growing.

Integrity is the most needed character trait today. As John Maxwell and Jim Dornan noted in *Becoming a Person of Influence*, nineteenth-century Episcopal clergyman Phillips Brooks warned,

> Anytime you break a moral principle, you create a small crack in the foundation of your integrity.

And when times get tough, it becomes harder to act with integrity, not easier . . . Everything you have done in the past—and the things you have neglected to do—come to a head when you're under pressure.

The Junior Reserve Officer Training Corps (JROTC) creed reads, "I do not lie, cheat or steal and I will always be accountable for my actions." Cadets at the United States Military Academy at West Point are guided by the timeless creed of "Duty, Honor, Country," with "respect" and "integrity" as their central fundamental values. Midshipmen attending the United States Naval Academy in Annapolis adhere to the Honor Concept:

Midshipmen are persons of integrity: They stand for that which is right. They tell the truth and ensure that the full truth is known. They do not lie. They embrace fairness in all actions. They ensure that work submitted as their own is their own, and that assistance received from any source is authorized and properly documented. They do not cheat. They respect the property of others and ensure that others are able to benefit from the use of their own property. They do not steal.

11

These concepts are not inherent. They must be taught. They must be learned. While Michael was in the eighth grade, his mother received a telephone call from the school principal reporting that her son had been involved in a fight. After arriving at the school, she learned that Michael had been fighting to prevent a special-needs child from being pushed into a locker. After this incident, he was given the nickname "the Protector." While Michael's parents certainly did not condone fighting, in this case, they could not have been more proud of their son.

During his freshman year at Patchogue-Medford High School, he often took a shortcut home through a wooded area. One day he came across several high school bullies tormenting a homeless man who had been collecting bottles and cans. The bullies had taken the man's bag and scattered its contents. Afraid, the frail-looking man cowered next to a tree. Michael confronted the bullies, one of whom said, "Aw, Murphy, are you going to start?" Michael replied, "No, I'm not going to start, but you're gonna stop." The bullies left grumbling but none confronted Michael, who began picking up the bottles and cans and putting them back into the bag. As Michael approached the man, he covered himself in fear. Michael stepped back and said, "It's OK. No one is going to bother you. I'm leaving. Your bag is right here when you want it." Leaving the bag nearby, Michael turned and started to leave. After walking several yards, Michael turned around and saw the man holding his bag, staring at him. Michael just smiled and waved, then turned and walked away.

In another instance while in high school, Michael noticed that there was a girl who always sat alone at the back corner table in the cafeteria. No one ever talked to her. After observing her for nearly a week, one day Michael took his lunch, walked over to her table, and asked if he could join her. Obviously shocked, the girl looked up at him but said nothing. Taking that as an affirmative response, Michael sat down and slowly was able to get her to engage in conversation. By the middle of the week, several of Michael's friends had joined them; and within a couple of weeks, the young girl was always in the company of others.

No one stands taller than when they reach down to help someone else up. Michael Murphy's character and integrity guided his behavior. From a very early age, he repeatedly demonstrated the propensity to do the right thing, at the right time, for the right reason.

As a result, in the first instance, he profoundly influenced his mother; in the second instance, both his parents and the principal. In the third instance, he influenced the bullies and the homeless man; in the fourth, the lonely girl. To Michael Murphy, it was never about him; it was always about others.

These incidents from Michael's life, which occurred many years ago, have had a positive influence on me, and I hope they will have the same effect on all those who read them. Phillips Brooks said, "Character is made in the small moments of our lives." Young Michael Murphy learned that leaders take people where they want to go; great leaders take people where they need to be.

Influence, Character, and Integrity: A Recipe for Leadership

A mantra of leadership expert and teacher John Maxwell is "Everything rises and falls on leadership." Michael Murphy was a student of both history and leadership. Leaders are effective because of who they are on the inside—the qualities that make them up as individuals, the qualities of character and integrity that can profoundly influence others. And to go to the highest level of leadership, people have to develop these traits from the inside out. People want to believe in their leaders; integrity certainly helps ensure that belief.

Michael Murphy was a student of leadership, with one of his favorite leaders being Abraham Lincoln. Consider the character test and challenge that faced our nation's sixteenth president. It was said that at the age of ten, Abraham Lincoln was at his mother's bedside when she died. Her last words to him were "Be somebody, Abe."

14

Many years later, despite threats of assassination, Lincoln arrived in the nation's capital, prepared to take the oath of office. By that time, seven states had seceded from the Union to form the Confederate States of America, with Jefferson Davis sworn in as its first president. Lincoln's predecessor, James Buchanan, had given up hope of keeping the country united and left Washington claiming to be the "last president of the United States." Lincoln immediately was faced with the realization that the Confederacy had taken control of all federal agencies and seized almost every fort and arsenal in southern territory, as well as in most of the Mississippi River region. The aging Gen. Winfield Scott, who many considered incompetent, led the scattered, dilapidated, and poorly equipped Union army of sixteen thousand men, many of whom were southern sympathizers. Despite being faced with the most severe of leadership challenges, Abraham Lincoln preserved the Union and became one of this nation's most revered and accomplished leaders.

Internalizing his middle school's motto, "With the Heart of a Lion, Do the Right Thing," Michael Patrick Murphy realized, like Lincoln, that a life best lived was one of selfless service to others.

In the following pages, we will study the most poignant leadership characteristics of Lt. Michael Patrick Murphy, USN and posthumous recipient of the Medal of Honor.

15

Notes

2

CONFIDENCE

As a military officer, Michael Murphy was always confident. However, his confidence did not begin when he entered the United States Navy. As a child, he learned from his parents that faith, hard work, training, education, and, most important, integrity would prepare him for the challenges to come; and when they did, he possessed the spiritual, physical, and mental resources upon which to draw. In *SEAL of Honor*, I recounted this story about his childhood:

> As a toddler, Michael's favorite book was Watty Piper's *The Little Engine That Could* . . . Michael knew the story by heart, and would slowly stride from room to room acting like a train engine, saying, "I think I can, I think I can, I think I can." After making the rounds through every room, he began running as fast as he could, saying, "I thought I could, I thought I could, I thought I could, I

thought I could." The lessons learned from this story carried Michael through some of the most challenging times in his life.

From his parents, he learned that leadership is a lifelong learning process, a process of disciplines practiced every day; disciplines that would shape his character. Leaders are made from the inside, and he learned that if he became the leader he wanted to be on the inside, he could become the leader he strived to be on the outside.

Great leaders exude confidence because they know who they are, not just what they are. They confidently demonstrate a strong work ethic and are well prepared because they have consistently chosen to make the character-building tough choices. In life, there are many things over which we have no control, but our character is not one of them. John Maxwell, in his book The *21 Indispensable Qualities of a Leader*, relates, "Action is the real indicator of character. Your character determines who you are. Who you are determines what you see. What you see determines what you do . . . you can never separate a leader's character from his actions." Character builds confidence.

After determining that he was going to become a Navy SEAL, Michael was invited to join the Recruiting District Assistance Council's SEAL mentorship program. The RDAC mentors soon noticed that Michael usually finished near the front in both his swimming and running workouts, but would always go back and encourage the slower swimmers and runners. To Michael Murphy, it was never about him, but always about others.

Despite having to miss a couple of monthly sessions, he tapped into his self-discipline and confidence to work on his own, allowing him to quickly exceed the RDAC's recommendation criteria. Great leaders refuse to take shortcuts in any aspect of their lives. Nothing builds confidence more quickly or completely than proper preparation. Proper preparation cannot be accomplished utilizing shortcuts.

Michael Murphy was accepted into Officer Candidate School (OCS) in September 2000 and graduated on December 13, 2000, as a newly commissioned ensign in the United States Navy. He was also accepted into Basic Underwater Demolition/SEAL (BUD/S) training, which he started in January 2001. On October 18, 2001, Michael signed his Fitness Report and Counseling Record, having successfully completed BUD/S. You also gain confidence each and every time you are successful at a task or complete an assignment.

Michael Murphy subsequently completed range safety officer, dive supervisor, and survival, evasion, resistance, and escape (SERE) training and was permitted to enter SEAL Qualification Training (SQT) before moving on to SEAL Delivery Vehicle (SDV) training.

Upon his successful completion of SDV training, Ens. Michael Murphy was promoted to lieutenant junior grade and assigned to SDV Team One in Hawaii as an assistant operations officer (a position normally filled by an officer two ranks higher), with responsibilities that included schools management, field training, and exercise planning and execution.

During the period July 3–10, 2002, Michael deployed to Central Command (CENTCOM), again as an assistant operations officer. As noted in *SEAL of Honor*, his Fitness Report and Counseling Record for second half of 2002 read in part:

> LTJG is a model SEAL Officer. Possesses the superior leadership, creative abilities and self-confidence traits to excel in any wardroom assignment. Hard charging Officer with unlimited potential. Unquenchable thirst for knowledge of NSW [Naval Special Warfare]. Recommended for early promotion, assignment as a Platoon OIC [officer in charge], and follow-on Post Graduate education.

Michael Murphy continued to gain confidence with each and every success, which occurred regularly. As recorded in *SEAL of Honor*, his

Fitness Report and Counseling Record for the period January 13–April 9, 2003, stated in part:

> LTJG Murphy is one of the finest junior officers I have ever worked with. A rising star in Naval Special Warfare, his work ethic, devotion to duty, and overall professionalism far exceeds that of his peers. Detail to only the most demanding assignments. Promote now!

Notes

3

ACCEPT PERSONAL RESPONSIBILITY

In today's civilian society, it seems that everyone is a victim. It is rare to find people who accept responsibility not only for their own failures, but also those they lead or supervise. In short, there is an alarming lack of personal responsibility. Too many elected officials, as well as those in similar positions of leadership, blame others for their own decision making, or lack thereof.

In April of 1961, President John F. Kennedy accepted full responsibility for the Bay of Pigs fiasco. It did not matter that the plans for the operation had started in the Eisenhower administration, or that intelligence failures directly led to the major foreign policy disaster just three months into his term. President Kennedy, a former Navy officer, stood before the nation and the entire world and accepted personal responsibility.

A military officer or anyone aspiring to a position of leadership must be willing to accept responsibility for his or her own failure or that of his or her team. A fundamental tenet of leadership is that regardless of their actions, leaders are responsible for those under their command. Air Force Gen. Curtis E. LeMay was once asked to provide a one-word definition of leadership. After some thought, according to Jeffrey C. Benton's *Air Force Officer's Guide*, General LeMay replied:

> If I had to come up with one word to define leadership, I would say responsibility. As a leader you are responsible for performing the unit's mission. If you fail, you are accountable for the consequences. Any unwillingness to accept responsibility for failure destroys our credibility as a leader and breaks the bond of respect and loyalty. Accountability also includes the requirement for discipline within a unit. A leader should reward a job well done and punish those who fail to meet their responsibilities or established standards. The former is easy, even enjoyable; the latter is much more difficult, but equally necessary. George Washington observed, "Discipline is the soul of an Army. It makes small numbers

formidable; procures success to the weak, and esteem to all."

As a leader, you may be able to delegate duties and even authority; but as a leader, the one thing that you cannot delegate is your responsibility. While others may be assigned to carry out certain tasks and duties, as the leader, overall responsibility always remains with you. It is when things go wrong that great leaders are identified. Great leaders will readily accept, without hesitation, full and unequivocal responsibility for their decisions, even when the results stem from the actions or inactions of subordinates.

According to William Safire and Leonard Safir's book *Good Advice*, which is quoted in the Army's *Leadership Statements and Quotes*, Gen. Bruce Clarke, USA, believed that "you must be willing to underwrite the honest mistakes of your subordinates if you wish to develop their initiative and experience" and admonished that "when things go wrong in your command, start searching for the reason in increasingly larger concentric circles around your own desk."

On December 13, 2000, having successfully completed Officer Candidate School (OCS) Michael raised his right and repeated these words:

> I, Michael Patrick Murphy, having been appointed an Ensign in the United States Navy, do solemnly

swear that I will support and defend the Constitution of the United States against all enemies, foreign and domestic; that I will bear true faith and allegiance to the same; that I take this obligation freely, without any mental reservation or purpose of evasion; and that I will well and faithfully discharge the office upon which I am about to enter. So help me God.

To Michael Murphy, it was never about him, but always about others. As a Navy officer, he understood that not only was he accountable to himself and those appointed over him, but also, and more important, he was responsible for those over whom he was appointed.

Had Lieutenant Murphy survived his last mission in the remote and unforgiving Hindu Kush mountains of eastern Afghanistan, there is absolutely no question he would have accepted full responsibility not only for the loss of his men, but also for the failure to complete their mission. Regardless of the reason, with each and every failure, responsibility must be accepted and borne by the leader.

Notes

_____

_____

_____

_____

_____

_____

_____

_____

_____

_____

_____

_____

_____

_____

_____

_____

_____

_____

_____

_____

_____

_____

_____

4

ABILITY TO LEARN ON THE JOB

Despite faith, hard work, training, and intensive study, each new position presents new challenges and opportunities for growth and development and, inevitably, mistakes—a few of which may be serious, even tragic.

While in Officer Candidate School and during the Junior Officer Training Course, Michael Murphy readily absorbed each of the lessons of the instructors, especially those who had been where he wanted to go. Even after becoming a SEAL, the learning did not stop for Michael—it only intensified.

Prior to their graduation from SEAL Qualification Training, Michael Murphy and his classmates received a handout from Chief Warrant Officer Mike Loo, the officer in charge that set down some basic principles to guide them as active-duty SEALs. In his handout, which is quoted in its entirety in *SEAL of Honor*, he admonished them:

Ultimately, you have a responsibility to the chain of command and to this country to be prepared to risk your life and the lives of your teammates as you go into harm's way to successfully complete the mission. You are accountable to do what is necessary to make this happen. That is the big picture. On a smaller scale, take your responsibilities seriously and be accountable for your actions.

Despite all of the precautions inherent in SEAL training, Lieutenant Murphy was involved in a near-fatal training accident while leading his team in a certification work-up exercise. Cdr. Todd DeGhetto described the incident in *SEAL of Honor*:

> Everything we do is high risk. Mike was learning. They were doing a closed terrain maneuver . . . They had a contact rear; a center peel was called, because there was no other tactical maneuver you could do. Everybody goes down into their field of fire. When Andy steps down into his field of fire, there is very tall elephant grass, perhaps five or six feet tall between Mike and Andy. As

the guys were center peeling back, Mike went down on his four power scope. As soon as he went down on that scope, he lost situational awareness, as Andy stood up . . . I saw Mike fire—I saw the muzzle flash, I looked at Andy's chest and didn't see any blood, I then looked in his eyes and I could tell he was hit.

As a result of this nearly fatal training accident for which he was responsible, Michael Murphy, following a full and thorough investigation, expected to be discharged from the Navy, or at the very least sent packing to the fleet. Cdr. DeGhetto continued:

After the incident, I sat down with my Command Master Chief, my Operations boss, senior leaders, my XO my Executive Officer, the senior guys especially in the training department that saw Mike and his abilities day in and day out . . . Mike made a mistake. He lost situational awareness for a split second, but he would never, ever do that again. I made the decision, I briefed my Admiral [Maguire] and he backed me up, because I told him point blank that Mike would never make that mistake again, as this was a mistake that you learn from.

Every single person I talked to recommended keeping Mike, putting him back on the horse and keeping him in ALFA Platoon. He was that good . . . We all make mistakes, and it was a mistake . . . Mike took this incident to heart and he learned from that mistake. He was a smart kid.

Despite mistakes, Michael had the ability to turn even the most tragic of circumstances into learning opportunities, ensuring that the same mistakes were never repeated. He knew as an officer and a leader that others depended on him to be the best he could be. To Michael Murphy, it was never about him, but always about others. He remembered the words of Chief Warrant Officer Loo's handout:

Never make the same mistake twice. You are your best critic! When you make a mistake or do something wrong, take it onboard and take it seriously. Be hard on yourselves. Do what you have to do in order to not make the same mistake twice.

Despite Michael Murphy's serious mistake during the training exercise, his Fitness Report and Counseling Record, filed by his commanding officer months after the accident, documented the following, as noted in *SEAL of Honor*:

> LT [lieutenant] Murphy was a LTJG [lieutenant junior grade] for 10 months of this reporting period . . . CONFIDENT, INTELLIGENT, SOLID PERFORMER. LT Murphy's care for subordinates and loyalty to superiors are second only to his relentless drive for NSW [Naval Special Warfare] knowledge and combat effectiveness.

All leaders make mistakes, but great leaders never make the same mistake twice.

Notes

5

COMMUNICATION

Gen. Dwight D. Eisenhower said, "Leadership is the art of getting someone else to do something you want done because he wants to do it." Many years before, President Lincoln realized that he could order his general in chief to move but could not make him do so. It is well known that Lincoln appointed and removed Winfield Scott, George B. McClellan, and Henry W. Halleck as general in chief before he found one that would lead the Union army into battle—Gen. Ulysses S. Grant.

Michael Murphy understood that the best way to get the men under his command to carry out his orders effectively was to involve them in the decision-making process. Communication with his subordinates was the means by which he could ensure that they would want to do what he asked of them. As an officer and a team leader, he most likely recalled some advice contained in Mike Loo's handout at his graduation from SQT, as noted in *SEAL of Honor.*

When you speak, you learn nothing; you learn only by listening. Listen, then speak, and speak from the heart. Take only those actions that make you a stronger SEAL or strengthen the teams. Think before you act. If an action does not make you or the team better, then don't take it.

On June 28, 2005, while leading his four-man team in the remote and unforgiving Hindu Kush mountains of eastern Afghanistan, Michael Murphy and his men captured three unarmed civilian goat herders after they were "soft compromised." Faced with a potentially dangerous situation, he instinctively knew to seek valued input from each member of the team. A frank, open, and honest discussion followed, during which there was reportedly some dissension among the team members regarding the fate of the goat herders. But seeking the input of others does not mean abdicating one's command. Michael Murphy was a United States Navy officer, with all the duties and responsibilities inherent to his rank, and he knew the final decision would be his.

Michael had the ability to talk to others, not at them. And he knew the difference between hearing and listening. He had the capacity to listen to others' points of view without feeling threatened or having his men fear retaliation from him. Listening to others, not just hearing them, regardless of rank is not a sign of insecurity or weakness, but rather one of wisdom and strength. His men were the best of the best—technical experts in their respective areas—and he wisely never missed an opportunity to seek their input. To Michael Murphy, it was never about him, but always about others.

At the same time, he knew when to end a discussion and make a final decision. Being a leader, he no doubt remembered Chief Warrant Officer Loo's admonition and, as described in *SEAL of Honor*, reminded his men of several key pieces of information:

- These three individuals were clearly civilian goat herders.
- If they aborted every mission in which they were compromised, no mission would ever be completed.
- The SOP [standard operating procedure] and ROEs [rules of engagement] for this situation were clear.
- If they were to eliminate these three civilians, who would do the execution, how would they dispose of the bodies and what would they do with more than a hundred goats

with bells around their necks?

- CJSOTF-A [Combined Joint Special Operations Task Force-Afghanistan] commanders were insistent on mission completion before command change.
- Shah's [the enemy leader's] forces were continuing to inflict U.S. casualties.
- This might be the best chance to neutralize Shah.
- This was their last scheduled mission before deploying to Iraq.
- This mission was why they had come to Afghanistan.

Consistent with those duties and responsibilities, Lieutenant Murphy led his men to the only correct decision—to release the goat herders and move to another location. It was the conclusion he had already drawn, but because he sought out his team member's opinions, they believed they had a part in making the decision.

All decisions have consequences—some even tragic. However, tragic consequences do not justify wrong decisions. Remember, a favorable outcome does not always indicate that the correct decision was made, just as surely as an unfavorable outcome does not always indicate that a wrong decision was made. In any moment of decision, doing the right thing is always the right thing to do.

Notes

6

ENABLE OTHERS

Because Michael Murphy was secure in who he was as an individual, he was not threatened by the success of others. While playing high school football, he was the starting receiver. However, he knew that his backup was a much better player, but for some reason he had not been able to demonstrate his ability during practice. Michael worked with him for several weeks and then went to the coach, encouraging him to allow his backup to start. Given the opportunity, the former backup proved himself, and Michael finished the rest of the season as the reserve receiver. To Michael Murphy, it was never about him, but always about others.

Michael's self-worth and confidence was not tied to his performance on the football field. As a developing leader, he began to recognize and understand that enabling others increased his self-worth and confidence and at the same time made the team better. What was good for his team always took priority over what was good for him personally.

Upon completing the Basic Underwater Demolition/SEAL (BUD/S) program and subsequent classes at the Army Airborne School, Michael attended the Junior Officer Training Course. During one of the sessions, as described in *SEAL of Honor*, the commander of Naval Special Warfare, Adm. Eric Olson, instructed Michael's class to "Empower your subordinate leaders to work at the full level of their authority. Encourage your subordinate leaders; train them, trust them, hold them to standard. Remember— the prime measure of your performance is the performance of your men."

A great leader is selfless. A great leader gives him or herself away by enabling others. As a Navy SEAL officer, Lieutenant Murphy made it a practice of mentoring and enabling others. He was not threatened by the performance of others because their efforts made him even better.

In *SEAL of Honor*, one of the men who went through training with and later served under Michael Murphy in Afghanistan stated:

> Lieutenant Murphy had a lot of confidence in his men. On one mission, he knew that I had completed the basic Emergency Medical Technician course, so when we had a guy injured, he called me forward and told me to take care of the situation. Another time, we were on a mission and he knew that I had

extensive training in land navigation and tracking; he again called me forward, had me look at some tracks, and asked for my assessment.

As word got around about how Lieutenant Murphy utilized his subordinates' skills and expertise, the enlisted men under his command began to hold him in very high esteem.

The process by which leaders enable others was best described by the late Vice Adm. James B. Stockdale, recipient of the Medal of Honor for his courage and leadership as a prisoner of war (POW) at the infamous North Vietnamese prison Hoa Lo from 1965 to 1973, in his book *A Vietnam Experience*:

> Leadership must be based on goodwill. Goodwill does not mean posturing and, least of all, pandering to the mob. It means obvious and wholehearted commitment to helping followers. We are tired of leaders we fear, tired of leaders we love, and most tired of leaders who let us take liberties with them. What we need for leaders are men of the heart who are so helpful that they, in effect, do away with the

need of their jobs. But leaders like that are never out of a job, never out of followers. Strange as it sounds, great leaders gain authority by giving it away.

A great leader also knows that he or she cannot succeed without the assistance of others. When there is success, it is due to a concerted team effort. Lieutenant Murphy gave all the credit to his team. In his last Fitness Report and Counseling Record prior to his final deployment, recorded in *SEAL of Honor*, his ability to enable others was recognized by his superiors:

> Selfless. LT. Murphy consistently shifts praise to subordinates and never ceases to secure professional recognition for fellow platoon members, including two NAMs [Navy Achievement Medal] and one command SOY (Sailor of the Year) in less than 10 months. His personable leadership style and mentoring methods have led directly to his platoon's high morale and 100% retention rate.

Notes

7

LEADERS ARE READERS

Regardless of how you define success, reading is fundamental and essential to anyone who aspires to be something more than ordinary. For those seeking positions of leadership, a daily reading regimen is critical. A little reading each day will result in the accumulation of a wealth of valuable information in a short amount of time. However, if we fail to set aside the time, if we fail to exercise the discipline of reading, then ignorance will move in to fill the void. If you talk to real leaders, you are sure to find that they are well read, and that in most cases their leadership positions are commensurate with their appetite for reading.

Of course, if you are reading the wrong books, no amount of reading will help. What are you reading? Is what you are reading stimulating your mind and thought process? Does your reading challenge you to reason more effectively? Does it impart knowledge and wisdom to help you learn, grow, and develop as a leader, or does it consist of mindless words on a page from someone's imagination?

Michael Murphy was a voracious reader and possessed an ever-expanding personal library. He learned early in life that reading was essential to mental growth. Most elementary, middle, and high schools have recommended reading programs. Unfortunately, all too many of these programs are voluntary, and so most students do not exercise the discipline of reading.

The SEAL RDAC program has a "recommended" reading list. However, the students learn in very short order that "recommended" means mandatory. No formal recommendation will be made to the Navy for BUD/S selection unless the candidate has completed the reading list.

The midshipmen at the United States Naval Academy have a comprehensive reading list that is divided by class rank and becomes more extensive as they progress. The Navy Professional Reading Program has a comprehensive list of titles that is divided into categories: junior enlisted, leading petty officers, division leaders, department or command leaders, and senior leaders. Reading and the disciplined implementation of a personal reading regimen is absolutely critical in the development of the knowledge, skill, and leadership characteristics so desperately required in today's military and corporate America.

Each branch of the military has its own extensive reading program list, as do most successful business and corporations. As quoted at the United States Naval Academy's website, Col. John Allen, USMC, then serving as the commandant of the United States Naval Academy, was adamant about the importance of reading and personal development:

> Learning our profession . . . the profession of arms . . . must be a lifelong and abiding pursuit for the professional serving officer. There can be no equal to, and indeed no substitute for, the officer who has spent a career immersed in the study of the art and science of war. An officer will likely spend no more than three and half years in formal, resident professional military education (PME) over a twenty-year career. With the preponderance of our time split between the operating forces, the support establishment, and "B" billets, we must assume the responsibility and provide for our own development. Unfortunately, unit level PME programs wax and wane based on commanders' predilections and experience, and operational commitments or other periodic interruptions. *Only the*

individual officer can be fully in charge of his or her professional development [emphasis added].

Michael Murphy had books on order when he was killed. One of the books was Lester W. Grau's *The Bear Went Over the Mountain: Soviet Combat Tactics in Afghanistan.* This book contains vignettes written by junior officers about their experiences fighting the mujahideen guerrillas in Afghanistan and served as a Soviet military textbook on mountain-desert-terrain combat. All leaders are readers, but great leaders are voracious readers who understand that learning is a lifelong process and that the best experience is someone else's experience.

If you want to know what our leaders are reading, I have included several extensive reading program lists in the back of this book. Use them. As you read each book, look for the leadership lesson(s) in each. If you are not looking for the leadership lessons, then chances are you will not find them. We usually find what we are searching for, so make sure you are searching as you are reading.

Notes

8

LEAD BY EXAMPLE

The best leaders need fewer words than most people because they lead with their lives. Lieutenant Murphy lived his life as an example. He always treated others the way he wanted to be treated: always giving them the benefit of any doubt.

He was always training and encouraging his men to do so as well, knowing full well that a pint of sweat saves a gallon of blood. He never asked his men to do something he had not already done or was unwilling to do. He trained and studied harder than anyone in his platoon, and his men followed him willingly.

Great leaders also know that the first one to become emotional in any confrontational situation loses. Michael Murphy knew that the sign of a great leader was to keep a cool and level head when everyone else was losing theirs, regardless of the circumstances.

SEALs are masters at controlling their emotions. Michael Murphy knew that becoming emotional during a time of crisis would compromise his ability to think clearly and logically. Despite being ambushed and outnumbered nearly thirty to one, Lieutenant Murphy calmly led his four-member team until he was fatally wounded on June 28, 2005, in the remote mountains of eastern Afghanistan.

One only has to listen to the audio recording prepared that fateful day when Lieutenant Murphy, in a cool and calm tone of voice, made his call for reinforcements, which ended with the words "thank you," to understand the wisdom of one of our early patriots, William Penn, who said, "No man is fit to command another that cannot command himself."

Just as Michael Murphy's men fought and died for him, he fought and died for his men.

LT. Michael Murphy, like all of this nation's warriors, was acutely aware that freedom is not free. Those who serve in our military understand better than most that everything has a price and that the price must be paid. Like the ancient Spartan warriors described in Steven Pressfield's *Gates of Fire*, "they know that their seasons are marked . . . not by calendared years themselves, but by battles . . . purchased with the holy coin of blood, and paid for with the lives of beloved brothers-in-arms."

Notes

9

LEAVE A LEGACY

Americans are fortunate to live in the greatest nation in the history of the world, beneficiaries of the living legacy left by those who have gone before us. Those who came before us left us the world we live in. Those who will come after us will have only what we leave them. The legacies we leave are part of the ongoing foundation of life, and we are but stewards of this world, with an obligation to leave it better than we found it.

Our Founding Fathers had a dream of freedom and self-determination, and left us the legacy of our Declaration of Independence and Constitution. Abraham Lincoln lived a life of selfless service to others. Martin Luther King passed down to future generations the power of a dream. The millions who have worn the uniforms of our nation—especially the hundreds of thousands who defended what we have been given and did not return—left us a legacy of freedom, and a better world in which to live.

It is an act of moral responsibility to leave a legacy. Because of the power of our lives and the legacies we leave, we all must assume the responsibility to create legacies that will take the next generation to an even higher level. This is what makes us a good and honorable people, living in a nation that Ronald Reagan described as "man's last best hope on Earth."

Dan and Maureen Murphy blessed their children, Michael and John, with the seeds of greatness. To those who knew him, Michael Murphy was one of the most selfless and giving individuals they had ever known. It was never about him; it was always about others. And because he was so giving of himself, he had few— if any—enemies. Those who met him liked him. Among his many attributes were empathy and generosity. By his example of constant self-improvement, he encouraged all who knew him to be the best they could be.

As noted in John Maxwell and Jim Dornan's book *Becoming a Person of Influence*, Pulitzer Prize–winning author Walter Lippmann wrote, "The final test of a leader is that he leaves behind him in other men the conviction and the will to carry on." LT. Michael Murphy passed his final test. His selfless act of heroism above and beyond the call of duty, like that of the legendary Spartan king Leonidas, made it possible for a lone survivor to carry on and tell his story.

At the age of twenty-nine, for his selfless actions above and beyond the call of duty, LT.

Michael P. Murphy was posthumously awarded the Medal of Honor by his commander-in-chief, President George W. Bush, in the East Room of the White House on October 22, 2007. Lieutenant Murphy's name, life, and heroism are now forever enshrined in our Pentagon's Hall of Heroes, in the hearts and minds of those with whom he served, and for all who have come to know his story.

Inscribed in a Wheaton College classroom are the words "He is no fool who gives up what he cannot keep to gain what he cannot lose." Despite our modern culture's obsession with winning and the rhetoric of subversion and moral inversion, was Michael Murphy's young life wasted, or did he know and understand something that many haven't yet figured out?

Michael Patrick Murphy clearly had it figured out. He selflessly and voluntarily gave up an earthly life he could not keep in exchange for an eternal life he cannot lose, demonstrating the wisdom many never achieve. Ever faithful to his creator, his country, and his creed, Michael Murphy bequeathed to each of us his selfless generosity, his empathy, and his wisdom.

The Navy SEAL Creed

In times of war and uncertainty there is a special breed of Warrior ready to answer our Nation's call. A common man with uncommon desires forged by adversity he stands alongside

America's finest Special Operation Forces to serve his Country, the American people, and protect their Way of Life.

I am that Man!

My Trident is a symbol of honor and heritage bestowed upon me by the Heroes that have gone before and embodies the trust of those I am sworn to protect. By wearing the Trident I accept the responsibility of my chosen profession and it is a privilege that I must earn every day.

My loyalty to Country and Team is beyond reproach. I humbly serve as a Guardian to my fellow Americans always ready to defend those who are unable to defend themselves. I do not advertise the nature of my work or seek recognition for my actions. I voluntarily accept the inherent hazards of my profession placing the welfare and security of others before my own.

I serve with honor on and off the battlefield. The ability to control my emotions and my actions regardless of circumstances sets me apart from other men. Uncompromising integrity is my standard. My character and honor are steadfast.

My Word is my Bond.

We expect to lead and be led. In the absence of Orders I will take charge, lead my Teammates, and accomplish the mission. I lead by example in all situations.

I will NEVER Quit!

I persevere and thrive on adversity. My Nation expects me to be physically harder and mentally stronger than my enemies. If knocked down I will get back up every time!

I will draw on every remaining ounce of strength to protect my Teammates and accomplish the mission.

I am NEVER out of the fight!

We demand discipline. We expect innovation. The lives of my Teammates and the success of our mission depend on me, my technical skill, tactical proficiency, and attention to detail.

My training is NEVER complete!

We train for War and fight to win. I stand ready to bring the full spectrum of combat power to bear in order to achieve my mission and the goals established by my Country. Execution of my duties will be swift and violent when required, yet guided by the principle that I serve to defend.

Brave men have fought and died building the proud tradition and fear of reputation that I am bound to uphold. In the worst of conditions the legacy of my Teammates steadies my resolve and silently guides my every deed.

I will NOT fail!

Notes

CONCLUSION

There you have them—the most notable leadership characteristics and the creed of the most celebrated Medal of Honor recipient since World War II. There are literally hundreds of books available regarding leadership theory and characteristics. Few address the personification of these characteristics. *SEAL of Honor: Operation Red Wings and the Life of LT. Michael P. Murphy, USN* does so. Study any great and honorable leader and I believe that you will find these same characteristics.

While political and military leaders change, our trust of and commitment to the less than 1 percent of all Americans who volunteer to wear this nation's uniforms must never change. All those who put themselves into harm's way in defense of liberty and freedom, as well as the families who endure their absence, deserve our unwavering gratitude and support.

While we all cannot be Michael Murphy, we all can be patriots. And when you stand before God at the end of your life, like Michael Murphy, you can say, "Lord, I have not a single bit of talent left; I used everything you gave me."

Let us honor Michael's life, service, and sacrifice by continuing his legacy of selfless leadership, empathy, and generosity, by becoming the absolute best we can be in every area of our life, and by encouraging everyone we meet to do the same. This way, the legacy of LT. Michael Murphy will transcend the generations.

SOURCES

Benton, Jeffrey C. *Air Force Officer's Guide*. 34th ed. Mechanicsburg, PA: Stackpole, 2005.

Department of the Army. *Leadership Statements and Quotes*. Pamphlet 600-65. Washington, DC: Headquarters, Department of the Army, 1985.

Maxwell, John. *The 21 Indispensable Qualities of a Leader*. Nashville: Thomas Nelson, 1999.

———. *The 21 Irrefutable Laws of Leadership*. Nashville: Thomas Nelson, 1998.

Maxwell, John, and Jim Dornan. *Becoming a Person of Influence*. Nashville: Thomas Nelson, 1997.

Phillips, Donald T. *Lincoln on Leadership: Executive Strategies for Tough Times*. New York: Warner, 1993.

Rohn, James. *Cultivating an Unshakable Character*. Niles, IL: Nightingale-Conant, 1984. Audiocassette.

———. *The Five Major Pieces to the Life Puzzle*. Southlake, TX: Jim Rohn International, 1991.

————. *Take Charge of Your Life.* Niles, IL: Nightingale-Conant, 1986. Audiocassette.

————. *The Weekend Seminar.* Niles, IL: Nightingale-Conant, 1999. Audiocassette.

Stockdale, James B. "Machiavelli, Management, and Moral Leadership." *Journal of Professional Ethics* (August 1982). Quoted in *A Vietnam Experience.* Stanford, CA: Hoover Institution, 1984.

United States Naval Academy Midshipman Reading List. United States Naval Academy, Stockdale Center for Ethical Leadership. Accessed October 7, 2011. http://webster-new.dmz.usna.edu/Ethics/midreadinglist%20page/midreadinglist.htm.

Williams, Gary. *SEAL of Honor: Operation Red Wings and the Life of LT Michael P. Murphy, USN.* Annapolis: Naval Institute Press, 2010.

LT MICHAEL P. MURPHY'S
MEDAL OF HONOR CITATION

The President of the United States in the name of Congress takes pride in presenting the **MEDAL OF HONOR** posthumously to

LIEUTENANT MICHAEL P. MURPHY
UNITED STATES NAVY

For service as set forth in the following CITATION:

For conspicuous gallantry and intrepidity at the risk of his life above and beyond the call of duty as the leader of a special reconnaissance element with Naval Special Warfare Task Unit Afghanistan on 27 and 28 June 2005. While leading a mission to locate a high-level anti-coalition militia leader, Lieutenant Murphy demonstrated extraordinary heroism in the face of grave danger in the vicinity of Asadabad, Konar Province, Afghanistan on 28 June 2005, operating in an extremely rugged enemy-controlled area; Lieutenant Murphy's team was discovered by anti-coalition militia sympathizers, who revealed their position to Taliban fighters. As a result, between 30 and 40 enemy fighters besieged his four-member team. Demonstrating exceptional resolve, Lieutenant Murphy valiantly led his men in engaging the large enemy force. The ensuing fierce firefight resulted in numerous enemy causalities, as well as the wounding of all four members of the team. Ignoring his own wounds and demonstrating exceptional composure, Lieutenant Murphy continued to lead and encourage his men. When the primary communicator fell mortally wounded, Lieutenant Murphy repeatedly attempted to call for assistance for his beleaguered teammates. Realizing the impossibility of communicating in the extreme terrain, and in the face of almost certain death, he fought his way into open terrain to gain a better position to transmit a call. This deliberate heroic act deprived him of cover, exposing him to direct enemy fire. Finally achieving contact with his headquarters, Lieutenant Murphy maintained his exposed position while he provided his location and requested immediate support for his team. In his final act of bravery, he continued to engage the enemy until he was mortally wounded, gallantly giving his life for his country and for the cause of freedom. By his selfless leadership, courageous actions, and extraordinary devotion to duty, Lieutenant Murphy reflected great credit upon himself and upheld the highest traditions of the United States Naval Service.

RECRUITING DISTRICT ASSISTANCE COUNCIL-NORTHEAST PROFESSIONAL READING PROGRAM

Couch, Dick. *Down Range: Navy SEALs in the War on Terrorism*. New York: Crown, 2005.

———.*The Finishing School: Earning the Navy SEAL Trident*. New York: Crown, 2004.

———. *The Sheriff of Ramadi: Navy SEALs and the Winning of al-Anbar*. Annapolis: Naval Institute Press, 2008.

———. *The Warrior Elite: The Forging of SEAL Class 228*. New York: Three Rivers Press, 2003.

Luttrell, Marcus. *Lone Survivor: The Eyewitness Account of Operation Redwing and the Lost Heroes of SEAL Team 10*. New York: Little, Brown, 2007.

Machowicz, Richard J. *Unleash the Warrior Within: Develop the Focus, Discipline, Confidence and Courage You Need to Achieve Unlimited Goals*. New York: Da Capo, 2002.

Mortenson, Greg, and David Oliver Relin. *Three Cups of Tea: One Man's Mission to Promote Peace . . . One School at a Time*. New York: Penguin, 2007.

Pfarrer, Chuck. *Warrior Soul: The Memoir of a Navy SEAL*. San Francisco: Presidio Press, 2004.

Pressfield, Steven. *Gates of Fire*. New York: Doubleday, 1998.

Sun-tzu. *The Art of War*. San Francisco: Long River Press, 2003.

Williams, Gary. *SEAL of Honor: Operation Red Wings and the Life of LT. Michael P. Murphy, USN*, Annapolis: Naval Institute Press, 2010.

UNITED STATES NAVAL ACADEMY
MIDSHIPMAN READING LIST

Fourth Class Midshipman (Freshman)

Fluckney, E. B. *Thunder Below*. Chicago: University of Illinois Press, 1997.

Jernigan, E. J. *Tin Can Man*. Annapolis: Naval Institute Press, 2010.

Potter, E. B. *Admiral Arleigh Burke: A Biography*. Annapolis: Naval Institute Press, 2005.

————.*Sea Power: A Naval History*. Annapolis: Naval Institute Press, 1982.

Prange, Gordon W., Donald M Goodstein, and Katherine V. Dillon. *Miracle at Midway*. New York: Penguin, 1983.

Remarque, Erich M. *All Quiet on the Western Front*. New York: Chelsea House, 2009.

Thomason, John W. *Fix Bayonets*. East Sussex, UK: Naval and Military Press, 2009.

Toll, Ian W. *Six Frigates: The Epic History of the Founding of the U.S. Navy*. New York: W. W. Norton, 2008.

U.S. Department of Defense. *The Armed Forces Officer*. Washington, DC: Government Printing Office, 1950.

Wolfe, Tom. *The Right Stuff*. Gordonsville, NY: Picador, 2008.

Third Class Midshipman (Sophomore)

Ambrose, Stephen. *D-Day, June 6, 1944: The Climactic Battle of World War II.* New York: Simon & Schuster, 1995.

Bowden, Mark. *Black Hawk Down: A Story of Modern War.* New York: Atlantic Monthly Press, 1999.

Bradley, James. *Flags of Our Fathers.* New York: Bantam, 2006.

Kennedy, John F. *Profiles in Courage.* New York: Harper Perennial Modern Classics, 2006.

Moore, Harold, and Joseph Galloway. *We Were Soldiers Once . . . and Young.* San Francisco: Presidio Press, 2004.

Moran, Lord. *Anatomy of Courage: The Classic World War I Study of Psychological Effects of War.* New York: Basic Books, 2007.

Potter, E. B. *Bull Halsey: A Biography.* Annapolis: Naval Institute Press, 2003.

Sajer, Guy. *The Forgotten Soldier.* Dulles: VA: Potomac Books, 2001.

Sears, Stephen. *Landscape Turned Red: The Battle of Antietam.* New York: Mariner Books, 2003.

Second Class Midshipman (Junior)

Brokaw, Tom. *The Greatest Generation.* New York: Random House, 1998.

Freeman, Douglas Southall. *On Leadership.* Shippensburg, PA: White Mane, 1993.

Kluger, Jeffrey, and James Lovell. *Lost Moon: The Perilous Voyage of Apollo 13.* New York: Houghton Mifflin, 1994.

Lott, A. S. *Brave Ship, Brave Men.* Annapolis: Naval Institute Press, 1994.

Manchester, William. *Goodbye, Darkness: A Memoir of the Pacific War.* New York: Back Bay Books, 2002.

McCain, John, and Mark Stalter. *Faith of My Fathers.* New York: HarperCollins, 2000.

Stockdale, James B., and Sybil Stockdale. *In Love and War.* New York: Bantam, 1985.

Webb, James. *A. Country Such as This.* Annapolis: Naval Institute Press, 2001.

First Class Midshipman (Senior)

Buell, Tom. *Master of Seapower: A Biography of Fleet Admiral Ernest J. King.* Annapolis: Naval Institute Press, 1995.

Campbell, Tom. *Old Man's Trail: A Novel About the Viet Cong.* Annapolis: Naval Institute Press, 1995

Heinlein, Robert. *Starship Troopers.* New York: Ace, 1987.

Lupfer, Timothy J. *The Dynamics of Doctrine: The Changes in German Tactical Doctrine During the First World War.* Washington, DC: Government Printing Office, 1982.

Myrer, Anton. *Once an Eagle.* New York: Harper, 2002.

Potter, E. B. *Nimitz.* Annapolis: Naval Institute Press, 2008.

Pressfield, Steven. *Gates of Fire.* New York: Doubleday, 1998.

Stillman, Richard. *General Patton's Timeless Leadership Principles.* New Orleans: Richard J. Stillman Company, 1998.

Stockdale, James B. *Philosophical Thoughts of a Fighter Pilot.* Stanford: Hoover Institute Press, 1995.

Sun-tzu. *The Art of War.* New York: Oxford University Press, 1971.

U.S. Department of Defense. *The Armed Forces Officer.* Washington, DC: Government Printing Office, 1950.

NAVY PROFESSIONAL READING PROGRAM

Senior Leaders

Churchill, Winston S. *Second World War.* Vol.1: *The Gathering Storm.* New York: Mariner Books, 1986.

Cole, Bernard. *Great Wall at Sea: China's Navy Enters the Twenty-first Century.* Annapolis: Naval Institute Press, 2010.

Holloway, James A., III. *Aircraft Carriers at War: A Personal Retrospective of Korea, Vietnam, and the Soviet Confrontation.* Annapolis: Naval Institute Press, 2007.

Knight, Robert. *Pursuit of Victory: The Life and Achievement of Horatio Nelson.* New York: Basic Books, 2007.

Lewis, Michael. *Moneyball: The Art of Winning the Unfair Game.* New York: W. W. Norton, 2004.

Manchester, William. *Goodbye, Darkness: A Memoir of the Pacific War.* New York: Back Bay Books, 2002.

McCullough, David. *1776.* New York: Simon & Schuster, 2005.

McIvor, Anthony. *Rethinking the Principles of War.* Annapolis: Naval Institute Press, 2005.

Mintzberg, Henry. *Rise and Fall of Strategic Planning.* Upper Saddle River, NJ: Financial Times Prentice Hall, 2000.

Pape, William Anthony. *Dying to Win: The Strategic Logic of Suicide Terrorism.* New York: Random House, 2006.

Schwartz, Peter. *Art of the Long View: Planning for the Future in an Uncertain World.* New York: Currency Doubleday, 1996.

van der Heijden, Kees. *Scenarios: The Art of Strategic Conversation.* Hoboken, NJ: John Wiley & Sons, 2005.

Department/Command Leaders

Baer, George. *One Hundred Years of Seapower: The U.S. Navy, 1890–1990.* Palto Alto: Stanford University Press, 1996.

Bossidy, Larry, Ram Charan, and Charles Burck. *Execution: The Discipline of Getting Things Done.* New York: Crown Business, 2002.

Friedman, Thomas L. *From Beirut to Jerusalem.* Garden City, NY: Anchor, 1990.

Kaplan, Robert D. *Imperial Grunts: On the Ground with the American Military from Mongolia to the Philippines to Iraq and Beyond.* New York: Vintage, 2006.

Kolenda, Christopher, ed. *Leadership: The Warrior's Art.* Carlisle, PA: Army War College Foundation Press, 2001.

Loden, Marilyn. *Implementing Diversity: Best Practices for Making Diversity Work in Your Organization.* Columbus, OH: McGraw-Hill, 1995.

Meredith, Martin. *Fate of Africa: From the Hopes of Freedom to the Heart of Despair.* Cambridge, MA: Public Affairs, 2006.

Monsarrat, Nicholas. *Cruel Sea.* Springfield, NJ: Burford, 2007.

Nevstaft, Richard. *Thinking in Time: The Uses of History for Decision Makers.* New York: Free Press, 1998.

O'Brian, Patrick. *Master and Commander.* New York: W. W. Norton, 1994.

Spector, Ronald H. *Eagle Against the Sun: The American War with Japan.* New York: Vintage, 1985.

Weelan, Joseph. *Jefferson's War: America's First War on Terror, 1801–1805.* Cambridge, MA: Public Affairs, 2004.

Division Leaders

Boot, Max. *The Savage Wars of Peace: Small Wars and the Rise of American Power.* New York: Basic Books, 2003.

Christensen, Clayton M. *Innovator's Dilemma: The Revolutionary Book That Will Change the Way You Do Business.* New York: Harper Paperbacks, 2003.

Friedman, Thomas L. *World Is Flat: A Brief History of the Twenty-first Century.* New York: Picador, 2007.

Hirsch, James S. *Two Souls Indivisible: The Friendship that Saved Two POWs in Vietnam.* New York: Houghton Mifflin, 2004.

Kagan, Donald. *On the Origins of War and the Preservation of Peace.* New York: Anchor, 1996.

Levitt, Steven D., and Stephen J. Dubner. *Freakonomics: A Rogue Economist Explores the Hidden Side of Everything.* New York: Harper Perennial, 2009.

Powell, Colin. *Golden Thirteen: Recollections of the First Black Naval Officers.* Annapolis: Naval Institute Press, 2003.

Reid, Michael. *Forgotten Continent: The Battle for Latin America's Soul.* New Haven: Yale University Press, 2009.

Schneller, Robert J., Jr. *Shield and Sword: The United States Navy in the Persian Gulf War.* Washington, DC: Government Reprints Press, 2001.

Sobel, Dava. *Longitude: The True Story of a Lone Genius Who Solved the Greatest Scientific Problem of His Time.* New York: Walker, 2007.

Toll, Ian W. *Six Frigates: The Epic History of the Founding of the U.S. Navy.* New York: W. W. Norton, 2008.

Leading Petty Officers

Gladwell, Malcolm. *Tipping Point: How Little Things Can Make a Big Difference.* New York: Back Bay Books, 2002.

Gray, Colin S. *Sheriff: America's Defense of the New World Order.* Lexington: University of Kentucky Press, 2009.

Heineman, Robert, Steven Peterson, and Steven Thomas. *American Government.* Columbus, OH: McGraw-Hill, 1995.

Hornfischer, James P. *Last Stand of the Tin Can Sailors: The Extraordinary World War II Story of the U.S. Navy's Finest Hour.* New York: Bantam, 2005.

Ketchum, Richard M. *Victory at Yorktown: The Campaign That Won the American Revolution.* New York: Henry Holt, 2004.

Lewis, Bernard. *The Crisis of Islam: Holy War and Unholy Terror.* New York: Random House, 2004.

McKenna, Richard. *The Sand Pebbles.* Annapolis: Naval Institute Press, 2008.

Melville, Herman. *Billy Budd and Other Stories.* Florence, KY: Wadsworth Editions, 1999.

Meredith, Robyn. *The Elephant and the Dragon: The Rise of India and China, and What It Means for All of Us.* New York: W. W. Norton, 2008.

Morrel, Margot, and Stephanie Capparell. *Shackleton's Way: Leadership Lessons from the Great Antarctic Explorer.* New York: Penguin, 2002.

Whipple, A. B. C. *To the Shores of Tripoli: The Birth of the U.S. Navy and Marines.* Annapolis: Naval Institute Press, 2001.

Wouk, Herman. *The Caine Mutiny: A Novel.* New York: Back Bay Books, 1992.

Junior Enlisted

Ambrose, Stephen. *D-Day, June 6, 1944: The Climatic Battle of World War II.* New York: Simon & Schuster, 1995.

Bradley, James. *Flags of Our Fathers.* New York: Bantam, 2000.

Card, Orson Scott. *Ender's Game.* New York: Tor, 1994.

Covey, Stephen R. *The 7 Habits of Highly Effective People.* New York: Simon & Schuster, 1989.

Cutler, Thomas. *A Sailor's History of the U.S. Navy.* Annapolis: Naval Institute Press, 2004.

Grafton, John. *The Declaration of Independence and Other Great Documents of American History, 1775–1865.* Mineola, NY: Dover, 2000.

Heinlein, Robert A. *Starship Troopers.* New York: Ace, 1987.

Hosseini, Khaled. *The Kite Runner.* New York: Riverhead, 2004.

Luttrell, Marcus. *Lone Survivor: The Eyewitness Account of Operation Redwing and the Lost Heroes of SEAL Team 10.* New York: Little Brown, 2007.

Morgenstern, Julie. *Time Management from the Inside Out: The Foolproof Plan for Taking Control of Your Schedule and Your Life.* New York: Holt Paperbacks, 2004.

Phillips, Donald T. *Lincoln on Leadership: Executive Strategies for Tough Times.* New York: Warner, 1993.

Ringle, Dennis. *Life in Mr. Lincoln's Navy.* Annapolis: Naval Institute Press, 2008.

AUTHOR'S READING LIST

Brady, James. *Hero of the Pacific: The Life of Marine Legend John Basilone.* Hoboken, NJ: John Wiley & Sons, 2010.

Bush, George W. *Decision Points.* New York: Crown, 2010.

Chernow, Ronald. *Alexander Hamilton.* New York: Penguin, 2005.

Couch, Dick. *The Warrior Elite: The Forging of SEAL Class 228.* New York: Three Rivers Press, 2003.

Covey, Stephen R. *The 7 Habits of Highly Effective People.* New York: Simon & Schuster, 1989.

Emerson, Steven. *American Jihad: The Terrorists Living Among Us.* New York: Free Press, 2002.

Flexner, James Thomas. *Washington: The Indispensable Man.* Boston: Little, Brown, 1974.

Franks, Tommy. *American Soldier.* New York: HarperCollins, 2004.

Goodwin, Doris Kearns. *Team of Rivals: The Political Genius of Abraham Lincoln.* New York: Simon & Schuster, 2005.

Giuliani, Rudolph W. *Leadership*. New York: Hyperion, 2002.

Hosseini, Khaled. *The Kite Runner*. New York: Riverhead, 2004.

Levine, Mark. *Liberty and Tyranny: A Conservative Manifesto*. New York: Threshold Editions, 2009.

Maxwell, John C. *The 21 Indispensable Qualities of a Leader*. Nashville: Thomas Nelson, 1999.

———. *The 21 Irrefutable Laws of Leadership*. Nashville: Thomas Nelson, 1998.

Maxwell, John C., and Jim Dornan. *Becoming a Person of Influence*. Nashville: Thomas Nelson, 1997.

McCain, John. *Why Courage Matters: The Way to a Braver Life*. New York: Random House, 2004.

McCullough, David. *1776*. New York: Simon & Schuster, 2005.

Phillips, Donald T. *Lincoln on Leadership: Executive Strategies for Tough Times*. New York: Warner, 1993.

Phillips, Michael M. *The Gift of Valor*. New York: Broadway, 2005.

Pressfield, Steven. *Gates of Fire*. New York: Doubleday, 1998.

Singlaub, John K. *Hazardous Duty: An American Soldier in the Twentieth Century*. New York: Summit Books, 1991.

Williams, Gary. *SEAL of Honor: Operation Red Wings and the Life of LT. Michael P.*

Murphy, USN. Annapolis: Naval Institute Press, 2010.

Wood, Gordon S. *The Creation of the American Republic, 1776–1787.* New York: W. W. Norton, 1969.

Wright, Lawrence. *The Looming Tower: The Road to 9/11.* New York: Vintage, 2007.

9/11 Commission. *9/11 Commission Report.* New York: W.W. Norton, 2002.

ABOUT THE AUTHOR

Gary Williams retired from the Ohio Department of Rehabilitation and Correction in 2011 and is a member of the adjunct faculty of Wilmington College. He began his corrections career in 1985 at the Marion Correctional Institution and transferred to the Corrections Training Academy in Orient, Ohio, in 1995, where he served as a training officer until 2002. While at the Corrections Training Academy, he developed a midlevel leadership program that received recognition in the American Correctional Association publication *Best Practices*. He transferred to the Warren Correctional Institution in 2002.

The oldest of five children, Williams was reared with a near-reverent respect for those who wear our nation's uniform. His father was a decorated Korean War combat veteran. Williams holds a bachelor's degree in human resource management and leadership from Franklin University in Columbus and a master's degree in public administration from the University of Dayton.

A previous work, *SEAL of Honor: Operation Red Wings and the Life of LT Michael P. Murphy, USN* was a finalist for the prestigious 2011 Samuel Eliot Morison Award for Naval Literature. He has six children and lives near Cincinnati with his wife, Tracy.

Made in the USA
Lexington, KY
06 December 2014